TARRAGONA
and province

Text, photographs, diagrams and reproduction
entirely conceived and produced by
EDITORIAL ESCUDO DE ORO, S.A.

3rd Edition

I.S.B.N. 84-378-1523-1
Dep. Legal B. 34008-1997

Editorial Escudo de Oro, S.A.

VISTA DEL PUERTO DE LA   CIUDAD DE TARRAGONA

The gate of Tarragona depicted in an engraving dated 1802.

THE ILLUSTRIOUS TARRACO CAPITAL OF HISPANIA CITERIOR

The city now known as Tarragona has its origins in the very distant past. Founded by the Iberians and later colonised by the Phoenicians and the Greeks, it was named *Caliópolis* "the beautiful city" by the latter. Hannibal was master of the city for some years and around 218 B.C. Publius and Cneus Scipio conquered the area which then went by the name of Cosse. From that date Roman Tarragona took on a historic role corroborated in the writings of Pliny, in his *Naturalis Historia,* where he states that Tarraco was created by the Scipios.

The city was quickly Romanised and soon became a port of prime importance for the Roman occupation of Spain. Tarraco attained high rank in the imperial organization shown by the fact that Julius Caesar and Octavius Augustus Caesar resided there for a certain length of time; the city later becoming the capital of Hispania Citerior.

According to tradition, the city was evangelised by St. Paul, and during 2nd century, Tarraco –with its 30,000 inhabitants– lived through a period of great splendour with temples, luxurious palaces, a forum, a circus, market, and theatre. It was girded by stout city walls and therefore possessed all the public amenities characteristic of a fully fledged imperial Roman city.

Tarragona fell into decadence in the 4th century when Constantine separated the Cartago and Galecia provinces from Tarraco. The Christianisation of the city was stained with the blood of the martyrs Fructuoso, Augurio and Galecia — the saints who were put to death in the amphitheatre of Tarraco in the year 259. Not long afterward, the Frankish and Germanic hoards devastated the land around Tarraco and tried in vain to take the city's Roman walls by storm. Much later, in 476, an army of Visigoths under Euric conquered and razed Tarraco, completely obliterating the Roman influence in that once powerful city. Outstanding dates in the history of the Visigothic occupation are the celebration of a provincial council in 516, the completion of the Visigothic cathedral, and the martyrdom of Saint Hermenegildo who was condemned by his own father King Leovigildo for having renounced Arianism; he was beheaded in the underground cellars of the Praetorium.

Moslem troops led by Tarik and Muza conquered Tarragona and its environs between the years 713 and 714. After some unsuccessful attempts to reconquer the city by the King of Aquitaine in 809 and by Guifred the Hairy in 888, Tarragona fell into Christian hands after the victorious campaign of Ramón Berenguer IV in 1150 and whole villages, castles and monasteries began to be constructed throughout the lands of Tarragona. In 1171 building was begun on the new cathedral in Tarragona and not far away, the Cistercian monasteries of Poblet and Santes Creus were being established.

Tarragona was annexed in 1220 to the crown of Aragón by Alfonso the Warrior, and subsequently its historical destiny became involved in all the vicissitudes of the history of Spain itself. Under the influence of the Catalan Renaissance, Tarragona has evolved considerably industrially and commercially since the middle of the 19th century, culminating in the development of the tourist industry which has made this fine Catalan city one of the most vigorous and dynamic of the capitals on the east coast of Spain.

Tarragona is a land where the earth produces rich generous wines. Its six wine-producing areas, Alt Camp, Baix Camp, Priorat, Terra Alta, Ribera d'Ebre,

A view of the central nave of the cathedral showing the choir stalls, organ and the main altar in the background.

The cathedral houses numerous chapels ranging from Gothic to Neoclassical styles. The photograph shows the chapels of Saint Thomas Aquinas, the Cross of Salvation and the Rosary, dating from the beginning of the sixteenth century.

Conca de Barberà and Falset are sources of considerable income. Strong wine and age-old history typify the personality of Tarragona.

Gabriel Miró, the Valencian writer, felt strongly attracted by the dionysic plasticity of Tarragona. The author of *Las cerezas del Cementerio* (The Cherries from the Cemetery) wrote, "The fields of Tarragona with their exultant plenitude, soaking up the blue. There is blue in the leaves which always look wet against the trunks of the trees, there is blue in the earth and it glows with the glorious colour of the ruins. The whole sky flows into the landscape like warm honey in bread, a blue light infuses all colours making them alive and vibrant. In the land of Tarragona away from the coast and through the pomp of pale gold and cool genista flowers, all the air is palpitating with the clear Latin quality of the Mediterranean. And this air of grace from ancient horizons leaves, in the sun of the corn and in the shadow of the pine grove, the emotion and whiteness of marble made into flesh. We see our narrow life illuminated and enlarged by a yesterday which smiled with all the smiles of naked goddesses. Incarnate land, inexhaustible, soul-earth feeding the olive tree, wide and solemn like an altar and beside this, the cherry tree, fragrant and dripping with fruit; marvellous land giving life to the walnut tree and a delicious chill to the hazel nut. Along the river banks are the live coals of pomegranate trees; the abundance of almond trees droops onto loaves of bread; palm trees rise up from enclosed gardens; the vineyard invades the plain and the gentle slope of the hills, the shining down-covered leaves of the fig trees join with the stiffness of the oaks; pine woods descend dramatically down the mountainside, and the locust trees drawing their claw-like roots from the ploughland, from the fallow, from the slopes, grow stubborn and strong down to the sea and in the dung of rocky places lie exhausted, restrained by the eternal limits of blue.

"Fields of Tarragona, womb of passionate landscapes and fertile earth, most glorious and prodigious mother."

Miró's sensual and luxuriant description, while out of historical context, nevertheless helps us understand the many natural gifts enjoyed by Tarragona which made it a place worthy of becoming the Roman capital of Hispania Citerior.

THE CATHEDRAL

Rightly considered to be the most important mediaeval monument in Tarragona, the Cathedral of Santa Tecla is situated on the highest part of the city, where, apparently, the ancient temple of Jupiter and an Arab mosque formerly stood. Work on it was begun in 1174 and ended in 1350 under the direction of Brother Bernart and Guillem Clergues. The building is the finest Spanish church constructed during the transition period from Gothic to Romanesque, and in the cathedral precinct there are several architectural styles existing side by side.

Its shape is that of a Latin cross, the long arm measuring 95 metres and the shortest 53. There are three naves, the central one of impressive dimensions is 17 metres wide and 26 metres high. The lateral naves are smaller, but in 15th and 17th centuries a double row of chapels were added to them. The cimborium is some 10 metres higher than the central nave.

The apse and the first floor of the cathedral built under Romanesque influence, have a fortress-like appearance. On the central facade with its serene beauty is a superb rose window just over the entrance and a fine sky light. An elegant Gothic staircase leads to the lovely portico with its slender concentric ogival arches beside which are inserted two square columns topped with a Gothic pyramid.

In the inside of this majestic church with its fine decoration, the original style has been preserved, the following being worthy of special mention: – the High Altar with its remarkable reredos in flamboyant Gothic style by Pere Johan; the sepulchre of the Infante Don

Partial view of the cathedral structure shown against its urban backdrop.

Detail of the main entrance to the cathedral.

A view of the cathedral. The imposing rose window over the main portal is one of the best examples in Europe.

The altarpiece of Saint Michael, a sixteenth century work by Bernat Martorell.

Juan de Aragon, with its magnificent recumbent statue carved in white marble surrounded by the figures of Saint Fructuoso, Saint Luis of Tolosa, Saint Luis of France, Saint Tecla and Saint Isabel, the Queen of Hungary; the priceless choir-stalls with their artistic Gothic seating; the organ, a fine Renaissance piece carved by Jeronimo Sancho and Pere Ostris; the tombs on the left of the choir-stalls where the remains of Jaume the Conqueror were kept from 1835 until they were returned to the monastery of Poblet in 1952; the Baptistery in an evocative Gothic style formerly dedicated to the Eleven Thousand Virgins, and the many interesting chapels inserted right and left in the cathedral naves.

The lovely cathedral cloister is worthy of its own description. Its style is a combination of Gothic and Romanesque elements. The naves are 45 and 47 metres long and the wide ogival arches are held up by more than two hundred artistically decorated marble capitals. The **Diocesan Museum** is housed in the cloister and has some interesting collections of Roman objects, tapestries, wrought iron, pottery, paintings, coins, manuscripts, vestments and other historical pieces making up an outstandingly valuable collection.

THE SEMINARY

This building, situated behind the cathedral, was built between 1883 and 1887. It has an interesting library with some 15,000 volumes, among them a valuable illuminated Bible which belonged to the archbishop Don Juan of Aragon.

In one of the courtyards of the Seminary is the beautiful St. Paul's chapel built in the mid 13th century and representative of the transitional period between the Romanesque and ogival styles. The chapel is built on a rock, from which, according to tradition, St. Paul preached during his stay in Tarragona.

Saint Paul's Chapel: the seminary courtyard.

The Archaeological Walk. The old stone of the monument stands as proof of the long and glorious reign of the Romans in Tarragona.

THE ARCHBISHOP'S PALACE

Close by the Seminary is the archbishop's palace built on neoclassical lines in 1827 on the site of the former Capitol, a section of the Roman wall being used for its construction. The so-called "Torre del Patriarca" (the patriarch's tower) is still extant. There are some interesting documents in the Diocesan archives, some dating from the 11th century and there is a noteworthy collection of 17th century tapestries.

THE ARCHAEOLOGICAL WALK

Tarragona appears to rise up from its strategic elevation like a fortress facing the sea, and still preserves part of the fortified wall that defended the former acropolis. This fortification carried out its important defensive role up to the beginning of the 19th century. The military value of the wall at Tarragona, in which Roman, mediaeval, and modern elements can be observed, has disappeared, but this has been substituted by its enormous architectural value. "In Tarragona, behind the archbishop's palace," writes J. Pin y Soler, "runs that portentous wall beginning in the Portal de San Francisco and leading up to Santa Clara. It is as solid now as in the time of the Crusades; as solid as in the days when it was attacked by Ethiopians, Phoenicians, Romans, Goths, Saracens, Christians and French. Imposing, majestic, thirty centuries were unable to breach it. Never was it abandoned to any aggressor or taken by force. The enemy entering the city always came from the sea. The city only becomes human for those who live there, who gain shelter from it and who love it, and although arrows, catapults, bombs, mines and cannon could not split the wall, this same wall in some strange way opens in welcome to the good priests and citizens who live in its shadow. These are the folk who penetrate the

Roman gateway.

The Gateway of the Rosary.

colossal mass with small balconies, windows, tiny plots of land, apertures for light and air. By growing old the wall has become peaceful, and instead of battlements and mortars, the wall is topped by sombre little terraces and in its crevices grow wild fig trees; ivy has been allowed to cover its gaps and jutting stones, climbing plants of all kinds hide its wounds and adorn it".

Today a broad walk has been made between the ancient wall and the fortifications, constituting the magnificent archaeological walk. From this uniquely evocative avenue in Tarragona there are some impressive views of the surrounding country-side.

The original length of the wall was some 4 km. At the present time there is only 1 km left of this fine fortification which contains three towers: the Archbishop's Tower, Cabiscol Tower and Minerva Tower as well as a large gate and five smaller ones.

Many descriptions have been made of the Iberian base of the wall which is built of very large, closely-fitted stones. The technique used to build it has always caused justified surprise among experts. For the base, colossal blocks of uncut stone were used and among these are some measuring 3 by 4 metres and weighing three and a half tons.

On top of this part of the wall are several Roman sections still gracefully erect, composed of bossed squared parallelepiped stones, and besides this are some mediaeval and modern reconstructed sections.

*Various corners
evoking glorious
Roman times in
ancient Tarraco: the
amphitheatre, the
statue of Augustus
Caesar, the Roman
gateway.*

A view of the walls and the Archbishop's Tower (fourteenth century) and the founders of Rome: Romulus and Remus suckled by the she-wolf.

Archbishop's Tower.

Front view of the sarcophagus of Hippolytus. A magnificent work dating from the third century exhibited in the Pretorio.

THE PRAETORIUM

This building is situated in the Plaça del Rei, alongside the archaeological museum and is known as the Palace of Pilate and the Palace of Augustus. It is a typically Roman edifice dating from the second half of the first century and reconstructed during the Middle Ages. It was the palace of the Catalano-Aragonese kings and its half Roman and half mediaeval design lasted until the building was blown up by the French in 1813. At the present time only the Roman walls remain with their bossed square stones, the most interesting part being near the staircase going down to the lower level of the Passeig de Sant Antoni and the section leading to the church of Nazareth. St. Fructuoso, the first bishop of Tarragona and St. Hermenegildo were both prisoners in the Praetorium.

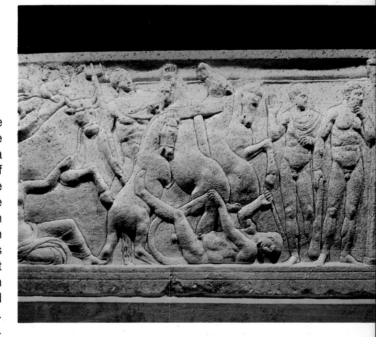

Side view of the sarcophagus of Hippolytus.

The impressive ruins of the Roman amphitheatre.

THE ROMAN CIRCUS

The remains still existing are to be found near the Praetorium and beside the city wall. The circus was of an impressive size – the area measuring 340 by 75 metres. It was oblong in shape and crossed the city from what are now the inner courtyards of the Baixada de la Peixateria to the Carrer de Salinas, occupying the space stretching behind the municipal palace. The most interesting part of the domed galleries that held up the tiers of seats which are still extant, is the one situated in the Parc de l'Enginyeria measuring 91 metres.

THE ROMAN AMPHITHEATRE

This was apparently constructed in 2nd and 3rd centuries and held some 24,000 spectators. The church of Santa Maria was built on its ruins in the 13th century. St. Fructuoso was martyred in the very amphitheatre along with his deacons Augurio and Eulogio in the year 159. Now the only remaining part of the formerly magnificent area of the Roman amphitheatre is a section of tiered seating and the arches supporting it. The length of the construction was 130 metres from east to west and 102 metres from north to south.

THE ROMAN FORUM

The ruins of what was the great Roman forum of Tarragona are to be found between the Carrer de Lleida and the Carrer Soler. The approximate area of the forum was 42,000 m². What remains now is a wide porticoed courtyard measuring 54.3 m x 14.3 m. The 24 columns supporting the roof of the portico, the figures in relief and the section of frieze along with other pieces are of great archaeological interest and allow us to mentally reconstruct the forum as it once was.

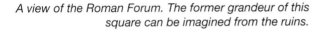

A view of the Roman Forum. The former grandeur of this square can be imagined from the ruins.

Two views of the early Christian Necropolis where numerous burial sites have been preserved in situ.

THE NATIONAL ARCHAEOLOGICAL MUSEUM

One of the most interesting museums of its kind in Spain, it has a fine collection of Roman relics of many kinds. It is housed in a magnificent building constructed in 1960 in the enchanting Plaça del Rei facing the sea. On the facade of the museum is inscribed the famous phrase attributed to Pliny: *Tarraco Scipionum Opus;* on top of the city wall where the new building joins the praetorium is the statue of Augustus by the Catalan sculptor Joan Rebull. The many different rooms of the archaeological museum are filled with remains from the megalithic wall, Roman sarcophagi, friezes, capitals, jars, bottles, figurines, glasses, sculpture, bows, and other Iberian, Greek, Roman or Visigothic objects. From this magnificent collection of some 25,000 pieces the following are particularly worthy of mention – the large mosaic of fish found a few kilometres away from Tarragona, the busts of Trajan and Hadrian and Marcus Aurelius, the statues of Venus and Minerva, an extraordinary mosaic known as "Head of the Medusa" and the sword of Jaume I.

NECROPOLIS AND PALAEO-CHRISTIAN MUSEUM

Situated close to the left bank of the Francoli on the Passeig de la Independència, the palaeo-Christian necropolis was discovered in the summer of 1923 during construction work on a tobacco factory. The importance of the discovery —it is one of the most important in the western world and the oldest in what was *Hispania*— was such that in 1930, a museum was opened on site to house the most important items.

The Archaeological Museum has many examples of exceptional interest.

*The Head of Minerva,
the head of Venus (a
Roman copy) and the
torso of Venus,
works among other
valuable sculptures
on show at the
Archaeological
Museum.*

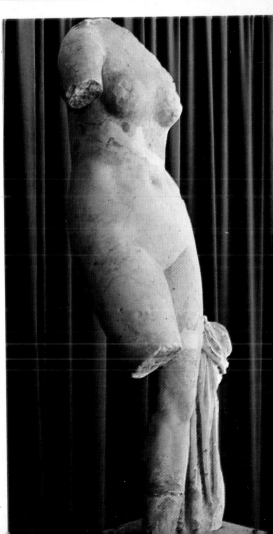

*Jointed doll dating
from the fourth
century, a valuable
and curious exhibit
on show at the Early
Christian Museum.*

The head of Medusa, a first — third century mosaic in beautiful condition at the Archaeological Museum.

A view of one of the rooms at the Early Christian Museum. The sarcophagus of the Pedagogue and the sarcophagus of the Lions.

Sepulchral mosaic of Optimus, a major work on show at the Early Christian Museum.

The palaeo-Christian necropolis, which was buried under 1.8 m of earth occupies some 200 m² and was in use during 3rd, 4th and 5th centuries. The remains of the Tarragonese martyrs Fructuoso, Augurio and Eulogio were buried there and as a consequence, the first Christians also wished to be buried there. More than two thousand burials, starting during the Visigothic period, were performed at the site. Numerous tombs are preserved *in situ* underground and in the area surrounding the museum building. There are many varieties from the simplest which are wooden or tiled as well as amphoras and other more elaborately worked examples including ancient funerary crypts. The museum contains many items found on the site including numerous household items such as the curious 4th century jointed ivory doll with found in the tomb of a young girl and marble sarcophagi, some of the most notable bearing carvings of lions, Saint

Peter, Saint Paul and the pagan of Sempronia. There are also jewels, ceramic objects, mouldings and ashlars and other items which together, give the necropolis extraordinary archaeological importance and make it exceptionally interesting.

THE CITY

Tarragona is, without doubt, a privileged city on several accounts: its splendid location, the treasures of its historic monuments, the marvellous light which illuminates the city and its enviably perfect juxtaposition of ancient and modern. It was not without reason that Junianus Major described it as "queen and goddess of Hispania, a glory of the Roman people comparable only to Carthage". This eulogy would now have to be completed by calling Tarragona the luminous pearl of the Costa Dorada.

If the visitor has already been impressed by the vestiges of imperial Tarraco and the cathedral which are described above, it should not be forgotten that there is still a great deal to see and do in the city. It is sufficient, for example, to soak in the view from the beautiful vantage point called the **Balcón del Mediterráneo** to be quite sure that you are gazing at a singularly attractive capital of great character.

The blue Mediterranean sea is closely associated

Partial view of Tarragona with the cathedral in the middle of the attractive town setting.

Fountain and gardens at the Balcón del Mediterráneo.

with the city. From this, one of the most spectacular coastal vantage points, 42 metres high and only 180 metres from the sea, you have the feeling of actually riding high over the waters. At your feet lie the fine inviting sands of Miracle beach and at only two kilometres distance those of l'Arrabassada and three kilometres distance, those of Savinosa. The **Rambla Nova** runs from the Balcón del Mediterráneo with its statue to the hero captain Roger de Llúria. A symbol of the modern Tarragona, this wide avenue which is some 700 metres long, is the centre of the nineteenth century development projected by Josep Criviller in 1855. Here you can admire the noble houses built during the second half of the last century and the Bofarull and Escorsa *Modernista* style houses. Other notable constructions in this district are the market, also in *Modernista* style and the Jesus and Mary school which contains a chapel with an altar by Gaudí. To the right of Rambla Nova, after crossing Rambla Vella, lies Tarragona's attractive **medieval city**. The names of many of the narrow winding streets are derived from the ancient guilds. Since a large part of the medieval city of Tarragona was built with material found in Roman constructions, visitors here can amuse themselves by spotting Roman stones and engraved marble slabs in the walls and facades of these old buildings.

In the medieval quarter, there are many notable buildings. Carrer Cavallers is one of the streets to have the most time honoured ancestry. Illustrious personages

Three views of the Rambla Nova which starts at the Balcón del Mediterráneo showing the monument to Roger de Llúria (in the centre).

such as Bernardo de Olzinelles who was chancellor and treasurer to King Peter the Cerimonious, Bernat de Saportella who joined the side of Juan II during the war of *Remences* in the 15th century and later, the marquesses of Montoliu, the barons of Foxà and the Castellarnaus all lived in this street in houses which are a testament to their noble lineage.

The most interesting of these old palaces is the **Casa Castellarnau Museum**. Built during the 14th and 15th centuries, it was the residence of Emperor Charles V during his stay in Tarragona and in the 18th century it belonged to the Castellarnaus. During this period the facade and the internal distribution were modified and the ceiling in the main hall was decorated with paintings on mythological themes by Josep Flaugier. The original majestic staircase which leads to the first floor and the harmoniously proportioned patio has been preserved. The other rooms contain furniture and other items dating from the 17th, 18th and 19th centuries. The museum's collection is completed with valuable prehistoric and Roman pieces as well as an ethnological and coin collection.

The **Plaça de Pallol** is one of the city's most beautiful corners. A magnificent Roman gate is preserved here. It used to lead to the Provincial Forum and now it contains a large Gothic window with two lights.

The **Carrer Major** is full of shops and contains interesting buildings like the old Town Hall – used by the council in the 15th and 16th centuries, the house of the Abbot of Poblet Monastery and the old Generalitat which also has a fine and noble facade.

In the Carrer de la Mercería stand the impressively graceful 15th century **Gothic Porches**. In medieval times this area was the market and to some extent it continues this tradition every Sunday when the weekly street market is held here with stalls offering antiques, antiquarian books, stamps and coins for sale. Stalls

The grand central aisle of the Rambla.

are also erected in the **Pla de la Seu** opposite the main cathedral facade in a square which also contains two interesting buildings, the Palau de la Cambrería and the rectory. Nearby, in the Carrer de les Coques lies the **Hospital de Santa Tecla** which is now used as the headquarters of the Tarragona District Council. Recent restoration has rescued this beautiful building which fell into disrepair as soon as it ceased to be a hospital. Built during 12th and 14th centuries, the lower part is romanesque and the

The Plaça Imperial Tarraco, one of the major road junctions in the city.

The clear blue waters of the sea seen from the city's splendid mirador.

upper part is Gothic. The facade contains a carving of Santa Tecla, but unfortunately, it is much deteriorated.

The **Modern Art Museum** in Carrer Santa Anna is housed in the Casa Martí which occupies three former noble houses dating from the 18th century. It has a neo-Gothic oratory and the main hall is graced with a cupula. It has recently been renovated and its collection includes sculptures by Julio Antonio and Salvador Martorell and paintings by Josep Sancho.

The Plaça de la Font, site of the Roman circus in ancient times and where the city council building now stands.

The evocative Gothic portals of the Carrer de la Merceria.

The Plaça del Rei, site of the Roman Praetorium and the National Archaeological Museum, stands at one end of the Carrer Santa Anna and at the other end of the street there is the Plaça del Fòrum with its remains of the 1st century wall of the Roman Provincial Forum. Leaving Carrer Santa Anna, crossing the Placeta dels Àngels, which was called the Jewry Square until the18th century, we enter the old **Jewish quarter**. The synagogue and the Jewish baths used to stand here and a large medieval pointed arch still stands. These little streets lead out of town through the **Portal de Sant Antoni**, a gate through the old Roman wall adorned with 18th century decoration.

No visit to this area of town can be complete without a walk to the Plaça de la Font near Rambla Vella. Again this is the where the Roman Circus used to be, the Plaça itself corresponding to the area covered by the arena. The **Town Hall** and the **Diputació**, or Provincial Council, are located here in a building which was totally renovated in the 19th century and where previously there were the Roman Circus dungeons and later a Dominican convent. The neoclassical facade, the work of the architects Barba and Rosell, contains images of Saint Oleguer and Robert d'Aguilló and medallions of Augustus and Adrian. The palace balustrade contains the busts of various Tarragonese notables and the majestic main staircase of the Town Hall can also be seen.

A view of the Carrer de Santa Tecla showing the cathedral bell-tower.

Facade of the old Hospital de Santa Tecla.

The pointed arches of an alleyway in the Jewish quarter.

Aerial view of the city and the port.

THE PORT

The importance of the port dates from the time of the Roman domination. It was modernised in the 13th century and at the end of the 15th century, a new quay was constructed. In 1802, the new facilities of the modern port with the lighthouse at one end were opened in the presence of Charles IV. At the present time there is a great deal of commercial activity in the port of Tarragona. It is one of the most important ports in Spain for the export of agricultural products and recently, with increasingly developed industrial areas, its traffic has increased considerably.

The varied aspect of El Serrallo, the fishermen's quarter, is part of the attraction of the port area which is lively and picturesque and of undeniable interest for the tourist.

A typical scene in the port.

The beach of Miracle lies at the feet of the city.

THE BEACHES OF TARRAGONA

The city is fortunate in having particularly attractive beaches near at hand. The nearest of all is Miracle beach which has very fine sand and is some 600 m long and 30 m wide sloping gradually down to the sea. Slightly to the north, some 2 km away with a regular bus service linking it to the city, is Arrabassada beach just off the main road to Barcelona.

Continuing in the same direction, some 3 km. out of Tarragona is Savinosa beach, 2 km. long, 50 m wide and also served by a regular bus service. It has fine pine woods to the east; then come the beaches at Capellans and Playa Llarga very close to Punta de la Mora where there is an impressive view from a 16th century watchtower.

HISTORIC SITES NEAR TARRAGONA

While the city of Tarragona itself is full of archaeological remains that are a testament to its splendid past, nearby there are also many monuments that prove that splendour was long-lived, lasting for centuries and reaching its zenith in Roman times. "Crossing the river Francoli," wrote the writer and traveller Crio Bayo, "the city of Tarragona comes into view, once a Roman colony and the principal city of the region. Here and there can be found proud vestiges of the power of Rome: the three massive gates in the wall, the amphitheatre, the temple of Augustus, the arch known as the Berà arch and the great aqueduct, magnificently preserved…".

This **Roman aqueduct** stands some 4 km from the city, towards Valls. Also known as the Pont del Diable (Devil's Bridge), it is a noble stone structure consisting of two rows of arches, with 11 on the lower level and 25 on the upper, a maximum height of 26 metres and a length of 217. It was built in the 1st century A.D. and is one of the best-preserved Roman structures. The aqueduct is a good example of Roman engineering which harmonises utilitarianism with beauty and simplicity of lines and proportions. It fits harmoniously into the landscape, the valley of the river Francoli,

The Roman Aqueduct.

The old square bulk of the Scipios' Tower.

whose waters it channelled towards the city of Tarraco. Its age-old stones seem to take on a new, fantastic life with vibrant colours when the rays of the sun shine on it – a phenomenon which is particularly striking at sunset.

On the right bank of the Francoli, close to the village of Constantí, is the **Centelles mausoleum**, a 4th-century structure of great architectural interest since it is a valuable example of Roman art in the latter days of the empire, and one of the most important funerary monuments in Spain. The mausoleum was erected on the site of an old Roman villa of the 2nd century, some parts of which still await excavation.

Dedicated to Constans, son of Constantine the Great, this mausoleum consists of a cuboidal base with an octagonal upper storey. Inside, there is a large circular room culminating in a dome decorated with concentric mosaics showing scenes from the Old and New Testaments and hunting scenes, and above, imperial dignitaries and the seasons of the year, of which only spring and autumn have been preserved.

The **Scipios' Tower** stands beside the old Via Augusta some 6 km north of Tarragona. It is a typical Roman funerary monument which, according to tradition, was erected in honour of the Scipio brothers, the founders of the Roman splendour of what was to be the capital of Hispania Citerior, although there is little to substantiate the association that has given the monument its name. It consists of three storeys, of which the upper is partly ruinous, and on which can be discerned representations of the deceased and some very worn inscriptions. The two carvings on the middle storey show Attis, the eastern funerary deity.

The **Mèdol quarry** is 8 km from Tarragona, between the Scipios' Tower and the village of Altafulla. It was from this quarry that the Romans obtained the stone for the building of imperial Tarraco. A monolith known as the "Agulla (needle) del Mèdol", 16 m high, testifies to the original level of the quarry. In some places can be seen the successive steps formed as the stone was cut from lower and lower levels. Now, in contrast

The majestic Arc de Berà built over the historic Via Augusta.

with the feverish activity that it must have seen in former times, the Mèdol quarry is a silent landscape, a sort of garden of worked stone.

Twenty kilometres from Tarragona, in the municipality of Roda de Berà, stands the majestic **Arc de Berà**. It was built in the 1st century B.C. with a bequest by Lucio Licinio Sura, consul during the reign of the emperor Trajan. It is a triumphal arch, typical of early imperial times, under which passed the historic Via Augusta. Harmoniously proportioned and elegant in style, it consists of a semi-circular arch crowned by a soberly-decorated cornice, flanked by two pairs of fluted pilasters with Corinthian capitals. The monument is 12.28 m high and 12 m wide.

Greenery and stone today make a curious garden in the old stone quarry of Mèdol.

The castellers, gigants and capsgrossos are the main features of the local fiestas.

FOLKLORE AND FOOD

Castells are almost certainly the most striking elements of folk tradition in Tarragona. These human towers demonstrate the technique, strength, balance and skill of the different *colles castellers* who gather in the main squares of towns and villages on feast days to take part in exhibitions that become quite competitive as they each try to build the highest *torre* or *pilar*. The tallest towers are up to nine storeys high.

The tower is called a *pilar* when there is only one person on each level, and a *castell* when there is more than one; thus, a *quatre de vuit* (four of eight) is a *castell* which is eight stories high with four people in each. The excitement of the crowd grows as the castle gets taller—the *cap de colla's* instructions can be heard above the din—and the climax comes as the small boys or girls who form the *pom de d'alt* ascend swiftly and the *anxaneta* crowns the tower, raising a hand in salute as the crowd bursts into applause. The *pinya* (cluster) supports the structure on the ground and on the second level, as well as offering protection against falls.

Another essential ingredient of local festivities are the giants, with their retinue of *capsgrossos* (comic figures with huge heads). Amongst traditional dances, the *Ball de Bastons* is particularly interesting. The local feast-days in Tarragona are Sant Magí, on 19 August, and Santa Tecla, on 23 September. Saint Peter, 29 June, is also celebrated in the seafaring quarter of the Serrallo. Also, Easter Week in Tarragona is particularly striking, especially the procession of the Holy Entombment, in which the hooded figures contrast with the faithful dressed as Roman centurions. As far as the table is concerned, Tarragona is part of Catalonia's fine gastronomic tradition. The sea provides a great variety of fish and shell-fish, and the plain of Tarragona is rich in natural products. Perhaps the most typical specialities, though, are *romesco*

sauce and the *calçotada.* The ingredients of *romesco* include garlic, tomatoes, specially-treated peppers, toasted almonds or hazel-nuts, vinegar, olive-oil, white pepper… But it is impossible to give the recipe for romesco because all cooks everywhere add their own *je ne sais quoi* to give their dishes that special touch.

The basis of the *calçotada,* a menu typical of Valls and the surrounding area, is *calçots*, tender, sweet, white onion shoots specially grown to be cooked over hot embers. Wearing the classical *pitet* (bib) to keep their clothes from stains, the diners take the *calçots* and coat them generously in a sauce called *salvitxada*. The traditional *calçotada* menu is completed with local wine, bread, meat, oranges and desserts.

Speaking of desserts, many suggestions can be made, such as *pastissets* from Tortosa, filled with jam made from gourds, *menjar blanc* from Reus, a cream made with almonds, hazelnuts and sugar, *carquinyolis* and *rifaclis* from L'Espluga del Francoli, or *bufats* from El Vendrell. The wines from the area are of high quality, particularly those from the Priorat district, which is an important wine-producing area, and Tarragona. Also very interesting are the wines from Gandesa and the anises and dry aguardientes from Valls.

The famous rifaclis of l'Espluga de Francolí.

Carquinyolis, a typical dessert at l'Espluga de Francolí.

PORT AVENTURA, A FASCINATING JOURNEY

Situated in Salou/Vila-Seca, Port Aventura is the first theme park in Spain. Visitors can make their way from the Mediterranean to visit the legendary cultures of Polynesia, China, Mexico and the Far West.

Covering an area of 115 hectares, Port Aventura offers a wide range of restaurants, shops, shows, games and 28 thematic attractions which are waiting to transport visitors to the most exotic and fascinating countries.

You can take a ride in a Chinese junk or a Polynesian catamaran or ride in a replica Central Pacific and Union Pacific steam train — like the one which joined the east and west coasts of the United States on 10 May, 1869. The first thematic area is Polynesia with its islands, huts and volcanoes which recreate the indigenous villages of Fiji, Tahiti and the Marquesas Islands with their luxurious tropical vegetation. Here, on an artificial beach, you can witness the spectacular dances

and rituals in honour of mother nature. The star attraction of Polynesia, however, is without doubt the Tutuki Splash. In boats travelling at 55 km/hour you plunge 17 metres down a Polynesian volcano.

Further on, you discover China. In this area we find, amongst other curiosities, Chinese acrobats performing in the Great imperial Theatre. China is also a paradise for those with a taste for excitement. The roller-coaster, called Dragon Khan, will pass into mythology. It is 1,285 metres long, has 8 loops, a maximum height of 45 metres and a speed of 110 km/hour — or the sensation to the body of a force four times that of gravity.

Accompanied by the sound of happy Mariachi band music you arrive in Mexico. In the midst of tropical vegetation you find a replica of the Chichen Itzá pyramid amongst other Mayan ruins. The big attraction in Mexico is the train in the mine, El Diablo, which takes you on a journey at top speed on board one of the wagons through a series of tunnels.

Further on the journey takes us to Penitence City, a

typical town in the Far West. It is 4 July 1876, Independence Day and a national celebration in the United States. With this atmosphere you can easily feel like one of the heroes in a film, having a rest in the saloon, watching the Rodeo, white water rafting in the Grand Canyon Rapids and even being washed down Silver River Flume on a tree trunk.

But Port Aventura is much more than this. The culinary specialities of each of the thematic areas, the street shows, the gift shops. Port Aventura lets you live your own adventure so get ready to embark on a fascinating journey to exotic lands which you will remember for ever.

Cunit. The Church of Saint Christopher.

THE TARRAGONESE COSTA DORADA

For 120 km, from Cunit, on the border of Barcelona and Tarragona, to Les Cases d'Alcanar, in the Ebro delta region, stretches the Tarragonese Costa Dorada, a coast with a variety of scenery, from rocky promontories and intimate coves to the beaches, some enormously long and others quiet and peaceful, as well as romantic pine-woods. The coast is blessed with the typical Mediterranean climate and the sun shines almost every day of the year on the fine, golden sands that give the Costa Dorada its name.

A view of Calafell showing the silhouette of the castle of the Santa Creu.

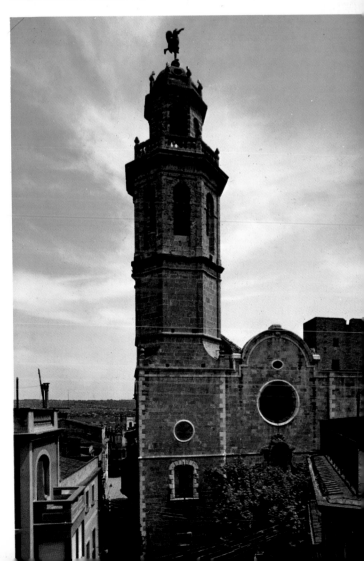

Sant Salvador beach.

Its natural beauty and its benign climate have made the Tarragonese Costa Dorada, like many other parts of the Catalan and Spanish coast, into one of the most important tourist destinations in Europe. Tourism, both domestic and from abroad, has grown and grown, radically changing the face of the area, which is today characterised by the proliferation of residential developments surrounding the old fishing villages, that still preserve their essential charm.

FROM CUNIT TO TARRAGONA

From Cunit to Tarragona the beach is practically continuous, and runs parallel with the old Via Augusta and with the rail line, which has a station or halt in every town or village. Beginning in the north, Cunit is the gateway from Barcelona to the Tarragonese Costa Dorada. The village is white and welcoming, and the beach is three kilometres long. There is an 18th-century church dedicated to Saint Christopher, built on the site of a 12th-century Romanesque structure.
Segur de Calafell is a good example of the effects of the Costa Dorada's tourist boom. Today, it is a completely self-contained tourist centre with all the necessary services and facilities, but originally it was a suburb of Calafell. Its beach, with shallow water, as is the case with most beaches in this stretch, is a kilometre and a half long.
Calafell is one of the most popular places with tourists, especially the area known as Calafell-Playa, which preserves the heritage of its past as a fishermen's quarter. The old town centre of Calafell is on the other side of the main road, and notable amongst its attractions is the castle of La Santa Creu (the Holy Cross).
The town of **El Vendrell** is some 7 km down the coast. It is the capital of the comarca (district) of Baix Penedès, and now an important communications nexus and commercial, agricultural and industrial

The high tower of the Church of Sant Salvador in El Vendrell.

Roda de Berà beach and a view of the Roc de Sant Galetà.

centre. It was founded in ancient times, and in the middle ages it was a walled town with five gateways, of which only the Portal del Pardo now survives. The parish church of El Vendrell is dedicated to Sant Salvador. It is a neo-classical building with a baroque doorway, built in the 18th century. The airy octagonal bell-tower culminates in the statue known as the "angel of El Vendrell". The church contains a remarkable baroque organ. El Vendrell also possesses notable mansions such as the 18th-century house known as Can Guimerà.

Sant Salvador and **Comarruga**, which began as the port and the sea-farers' district of El Vendrell, are now important tourist centres. The magnificent beach stretches from Sant Salvador to Francàs. Comarruga also has a well-equipped marina.

Another of Sant Salvador's features of interest is the Pau Casals house-museum. This was the home which the family of the brilliant cellist, born in El Vendrell, built on the sea front. It contains several rooms preserved as they were at the time and a number of objects associated with the musician are on display, as well as paintings and sculptures of Catalan artists who were friends of Casals. Nearby is the recently-built Pau Casals auditorium, now one of the liveliest musical centres in Catalonia.

Past the village of **Roda de Berà**, where the majestic Arc de Berà stands, can be seen on a small headland the curious development of **Roc de Sant Gaietà**, whose houses reproduce the styles of many parts of Spain.

Torredembarra was until the 18th century an important fishing port, since the customs were based there before they were relocated in Tarragona. Its beach is now one of the most popular on the Costa Dorada.

The Neoclassical parish church at Torredembarra.

The gateway to the castle at Torredembarra, built in the twelfth century and restored in the seventeenth century.

Three views of Altafulla: the sanctuary of Saint Anthony, a typical corner in the old quarter and the castle of the Marquises of Tamarit.

Remains of the old town walls are preserved, as well as part of a medieval castle.

Altafulla, "Palfuriana" in the 11th century, is dominated by the castle and the church of Sant Martí. The old quarter and the oratory of Sant Antoni de Altafulla also testify to its history. Not far away, beside the sea, rises Tamarit Castle. It seems the original structure dates back to the 11th century, but it was completely rebuilt by the Deerings from north America early in the 20th century as a family residence. In olden times the castle suffered the attacks of corsairs and pirates, who were a frequent menace for many ports of the Costa Dorada.

FROM TARRAGONA TO THE EBRO DELTA

While as we have seen, the beaches from Cunit to Tamarit are practically uninterrupted, the relief of the Costa Dorada from the mouth of the river Gaià to the Salou–Cambrils area, including the city of Tarragona is more abrupt, characterised by an alternation of rocky promontories with beaches and intimate coves, which, together with the leafy pine-woods, make this part of the coast particularly beautiful.

Before reaching Salou, only 5 km from Tarragona, we come to **La Pineda**, a large beach over 4 km long beside which an important and popular tourist centre has grown up. The sand is very fine and the clear

An aerial view of the beach at Salou.

water is quite shallow. On the outskirts is the sanctuary of Our Lady of Pineda, where traditionally the people of the neighbouring village of Vila-Seca go to eat the popular *mona de Pasqua.*

After La Pineda, the road to Salou that hugs the coast makes an exceptionally attractive drive. Alternating with the summer homes, the leafy woods dominate the view and, between the rocks by the sea, little coves open up, ideal spots for sea angling. This is the Cape of Salou, and on one of its higher points a lighthouse has been built. The beautiful, intimate coves are known as El Recó de Salou, Els Crancs (crabs) and La Font.

Beyond Platja Llarga and Platja dels Capellans, now quite heavily built up, the town centre of **Salou** stretches along its large beach. Salou is now one of the most important tourist centres on the Mediterranean and attracts thousands of holiday-makers every year. The all-year-round population is, nonetheless, considerable.

Salou became popular as "Reus beach" in the late 19th century, when people from Reus built summer homes there. Later, especially as a result of the tourist boom in the sixties, the beach became fashionable and the town has never ceased to grow, albeit in an orderly way. What was once the "Reus beach" is now known as "Europe beach" on account of its international fame and its cosmopolitan character.

The broad seafront promenade is one of Salou's main attractions.

However, the origins of the town go back to before the Christian era when, it seems, the Phocians founded a colony here by the name of Salauris. Historically it was one of the most important trading ports on the Catalan coast. A monument to King Jaume I, the Conqueror on the promenade is a reminder of the fact that it was from here that the royal fleet left in 1229 to conquer Mallorca. The Torre Vella (Old Tower) built in the 16th century by Pedro de Cardona for defence against pirates, still stands sentry by the beach. It is the oldest surviving building in Salou. Other items of architectural interest are the Renaissance-style church, the remains of some defensive towers, the Palau Sicart and several summer residences in Modernista style. However, its closeness to Reus and Tarragona makes it a fine centre for visiting the province's most important ancient monuments, museums and buildings of interest.

Small bays strung out along the low cliffs of Cap de Salou.

An aerial view of La Pineda beach.

The modern town of Salou is organised along the seaside promenade, a broad, palm-lined avenue which is bustling all day. In the evening, the illuminated fountain with its musical accompaniment is one of the chief attractions of this pleasant walk. Salou also has an excellent marina and a municipal stadium. The beach is 3 km long. The town's extensive tourist facilities as in Pineda, include shops, camp sites, apartments, hotels and restaurants. As for food typical of the Costa Dorada, the most interesting recipes are perhaps fish dishes such as the tasty *suquet de peix* and *arrosejats,* which will certainly please the finest palate.

The exciting fish auctions, held after the boats come in at many places on the Costa Dorada, such as **Cambrils de Mar**, are another lure for visitors. Cambrils de Mar, a traditional trading and fishing port since the 13th century, is now also an important tourist centre, whose harbour-side restaurants are famous for their excellent fish and sea-food specialities. Cambrils is divided into two zones of which the inland one is traditionally devoted to agriculture. Within the municipal boundary is Parc Samà, which was built in the 19th century and includes a furnished mansion and large, beautifully cared-for gardens.

Not far from Cambrils is **Miami Platja**, a pleasant modern tourist development with a beach one and a half kilometres long bathed by shallow waters, and then **l'Hospitalet de l'Infant**, off whose beaches, also with shallow water, fish abound.

The seafront promenade at Cambrils de Mar looks inviting for a pleasant stroll.

Near **l'Ametlla de Mar**, a small fishing port surrounded by pine-woods, there are several coves with beaches of coarse sand, the most beautiful of which are perhaps Forn and Sant Roc. Public fish auctions are still held. Beyond l'Ametlla de Mar the Costa Dorada gives way to the regions of the Ebro delta.

The port at Ametllà de Mar.

Tortosa: the Pont dels Muts and the Roser church.

TORTOSA AND THE EBRO DELTA

Tortosa, the capital of the Baix Ebre district, stands astride the Ebro river. Because of its strategic riverside site, the city has become one of the most illustrious and important in Catalonia, both because of its history and of its continuing growth as a commercial and industrial centre. Inhabited since ancient times, the Romans founded the flourishing colony of Dertosa here. The splendour of the city continued under the Visigoths and then the Moors, who were its masters from the 8th to the 12th century. After the Reconquest the city was granted a charter of privileges and its importance continued to grow throughout the mediaeval period. The castle of the Suda, started in the 10th century, is a relic of the Moorish period and parts of the original structure are still preserved. Apart from being a military fortress, it was also a residence of the monarchs of the Catalano-Aragonese dynasty. From the castle, now a Parador, there is a splendid view over the city and the Ebro valley.

The old centre of Tortosa is listed in its entirety as being of historical and architectural interest, there are a number of striking buildings, notably the cathedral, considered to be one of the most beautiful Gothic cathedrals in Spain. Work on it began the mid 14th century on the site of a Roman temple, while the 18th-century west end has baroque overtones. Inside can be found the image of the city's patron saint, Nuestra Señora de la Cinta, a richly-carved baroque work, as

well as retables of great artistic worth and a fine set of choir stalls. The cloister contains Romanesque and Gothic elements.

Near the cathedral there are other buildings of great interest: the bishop's palace, the Despuig mansion, and the Oriol, or Oliver el Boteller, Palace, all of them Gothic in style. The winding streets of the old town evoke Tortosa's mediaeval period, as does the former Jewish quarter (the Remolins district) built in the 12th century outside the walls. The Exchange has its origins at the beginning of the 14th century. The Sant Lluís college is Renaissance in style, with baroque elements.

The 16th-century church of Sant Domènec now contains the municipal archive and museum, which possesses an extremely interesting collection of documents concerning the city, particularly from the mediaeval period, such as the Carta de la Població (12th century) and the manuscript of the customs of Tortosa (13th century, as well as many archaeological remains. Tortosa's other museum is the cathedral museum.

Amposta, on the right bank of the Ebro, is an important agricultural and industrial centre and the capital of the Montsià district. The tall chimneys of the rice mils and the gentle hills with their olive groves and vineyards stretching up towards the mountains, blend into a single landscape. The suspension bridge, opened in 1919, and the parish church of Santa Maria de l'Assumpció (18th to 19th centuries) are the main items of architectural interest in this welcoming town. The municipal museum contains various archaeological items found in the district, as well as local ornithological and ethnological material.

The **Ebro delta** can be approached either through Amposta or along the coast. With its beautiful scenery, the Ebro delta is a peninsula covering more than

Panoramic view of Amposta with the bridge over the River Ebro in the foreground.

Broad stretches of beaches finally join the delta to the sea.

250 square kilometres and is the second largest wetland in the western Mediterranean. It was declared a National Park in the eighties, thus fulfilling the aspirations of the people of the area who sought to preserve its extraordinarily important ecosystem. In **Deltebre** there is an ecology museum and information centre. From the village public ferries operate every day, crossing the river in about five minutes. Other highly recommendable forms of transport are car or bicycle, to discover, little by little, all the immense natural beauty of the delta.

The delta is a very varied area; the abundant vegetation of the orchards alternates with great stretches of rice-paddies and, as the river approaches the sea, and the water is already salty, long beaches. The appearance of the rice-paddies varies according to the time of year: flooded in spring, green in summer, they take on a curious dark shade in autumn and winter.

The Park is also fascinating for the richness of its fauna, particularly birds, of which over 300 species have been catalogued, with large breeding colonies. The delta is also a refuge for migrating birds. All sorts of species can be seen arriving over the rice paddies, especially in the evening: ducks, herons, gulls, flamingos, moorhens, and many others. Fish, too, is abundant. A visit here should be rounded off by a meal in one of the local restaurants to savour the specialities of the delta, such as rice or shell-fish.

A noteworthy sight on the left bank is the sanctuary of

Ricefields and various bird species are an unmistakable part of the landscape of the River Ebro delta.

Mare de Déu de l'Aldea, rebuilt in the 18th century, which stands very close to Deltebre, to which the hamlets of Jesus i Maria and La Cava also belong, as does the Riumar estate. The Punta del Fangar includes the Marquesa beach and the Fangar light-house. Traces of earlier times can be seen on the island of Buda, where the grand Casa de Buda rises, with its chapel alongside.

On the right bank can be found the natural meres of La Tancada and L'Escanyissada, exceptional habitats for birds and fish, although there is also agricultural activity here too. The beaches of El Trabucador and Punta de la Banya, with its nearby salt pans, are of very fine sand and very long. El Trabucador beach is in fact 10 km long, and it can be covered by waves if there is a storm or a heavy sea.

The broad Alfacs bay, which enjoys the natural shelter of the Punta de la Banya, is a stretch of warm, calm water ideal for various water sports. Sailing boats and wind-surfers form a part of the scenery, and the area is popular with scuba-divers. The river Ebro itself, here wide and calm, is also a fine place for water sports, of which rowing is the most traditional.

Sant Carles de la Ràpita stands at the entrance to the Port del Alfacs, south of the Ebro delta, between the mountains and the sea. A remarkable feature of this pretty fishing village is the oval Plaça de Carles III, of enormous size for such a small place. Originally it was part of this king's plans to develop Sant Carles de la Ràpita into a port of international importance, but when the king died in 1788 this grand project came to nothing. Here stands the parish church, a new building erected on the site of one which was demolished after the Civil War.

The port of Sant Carles de la Ràpita, which was historically very important, is nowadays busy with fishing vessels and leisure craft. Around here, amongst

View of the beach, the centre of Sant Carles de la Ràpita and the parish church.

The sanctuary of El Remei at Alcanar.

other sea-food dishes, the delicious *llagostinada* can be enjoyed, a dish for which the area is famous.

Alcanar is the last settlement on the Tarragonese coast, marking the end of the Costa Dorada and the start of the Costa de Azahar, in the adjacent province of Castelló de la Plana. The old centre is inland, and possesses interesting architectural remains, such as a Moorish tower and the sanctuary of El Remei. The port of **Les Cases d'Alcanar** has in recent years developed an important tourist industry. Apart from the delights of the table, the village owes its popularity to the nine kilometres of beach with fairly coarse sand and pleasant, fairly shallow water, that stretch out at the foot of the Serra del Montsià.

The port at Les Cases d'Alcanar.

The high bell-tower of Saint Peter's church reaches a height of 63 m.

A picture of Nuestra Señora de la Misericordia, the patron saint of Reus.

REUS

Standing 13 km from Tarragona and 8 from the coast, Reus dominates a broad, rich valley that stretches between the mountains and the sea. The town is of very ancient origin, and the beautiful surrounding countryside was praised by Martial and other illustrious Classical poets. Since the middle ages it has been the commercial capital *par excellence* of the province being particularly famous in the late 18th century when the expression Reus–Paris–London became popular, since hazelnuts from Reus and the famous aguardiente were much prized in the markets of Paris and London.

The town has grown enormously in recent decades, but the centre still bears the characteristic stamp of the nineteenth century. From mediaeval times there are remnants of the old Castell del Cambrer, such as a few rooms with pointed arches. The church of Saint Peter was begun in 1512. Notable features are its simple Renaissance doorway, the beautiful rose window, the ogival windows and the bell-tower, an airy, hexagonal structure five storeys high that culminates in a pinnacle. Inside are the tombs of the first marquis of Tamarit and of his daughter Gertrudis.

Other buildings of interest are the Bofarull palace, with its Churrigueresque, or exuberant baroque facade, and the old convent of Sant Francesc, in

Reus has some beautiful Modernist buildings. These pictures show two works by Domènech i Montaner: the Pere Mata Institute and the Casa Navàs.

Graeco-Roman style. The Teatre Fortuny and the Cercle de la Lectura are the main centres of the town's cultural life. The Cercle de la Lectura was founded in 1859, and has exhibition rooms, a conference hall, a museum, a theatre and a well-stocked library of over 60,000 books.

The *Modernista* buildings in Reus deserve special mention, particularly the Institut Pere Mata and the Casa Navàs, both the work of Lluís Domènech i Montaner. The former, a psychiatric hospital, is on the outskirts, while the Casa Navàs, commissioned from the architect by the family of the same name, stands in the central Mercadal square. The Casa Navàs is striking not only for its exterior, but also because of its rich, exquisitely-decorated interior. Other *Modernista* architects who worked in Reus included Joan Rubió and Pere Caselles, both of them natives of the town, as indeed was Antoni Gaudí himself, although he, the greatest figure of the movement, never built anything here in the capital of the Baix Camp district.

Reus has several museums, including the district museum in the *Modernista* style, Casa Rull, which has rooms devoted to the history and customs of Reus and the surrounding area, and a rich collection of ceramics. There are paintings and sculptures by various artists, notably Marià Fortuny, a famous son of the town. The Salvador Vilaseca archaeological museum, in the former Banco de España, another *Modernista* building, contains an extremely important collection from prehistoric to Roman times.

Two kilometres from Reus there stands the sanctuary of Nuestra Señora de la Misericordia, in Renaissance style, which contains the image of the patron of the city, who, according to popular legend, appeared on 25 September 1592 to a shepherd-girl called Isabel Blasora to announce that she would put an end to the epidemic of plague that was devastating the population.

View of Valls showing the tower of Saint John the Baptist's church.

VALLS

Valls, capital of the district of l'Alt Camp, has been able to combine its traditional role as an important Tarragonese industrial centre with a thriving industrial present. Some remains of the town walls are a testament to its historic past. Streets such as those of Castell, Carme or Camisseria, the winding streets of the Call (former Jewish quarter), and the colonnaded squares of l'Oli and El Blat, are evocative of mediaeval times. In the Plaça del Blat stands the town hall, with a beautiful late-19th-century facade. Inside there is a majestic gallery of illustrious citizens of Valls, including the novelist Narcis Oller, a leading figure of the *Noucentista* artistic movement.

Valls parish church is dedicated to Saint John the Baptist. It was built in the 16th century and the elegant bell-tower, which is 76 m high, was added in 1895. It contains retables of great artistic value and the image of the Virgen de la Candelaria, patron of Valls, carved in the 13th century. Other points of interest are the Capilla de la Roser, with its fascinating tiles commemorating the battle of Lepanto, and the city museum, with an important collection of 19th and 20th century Catalan painting.

Superb aguardientes and the delicious *calçotada* have made Valls justly famous, as have its *castellers;* it is not for nothing that the town has received the honorary title of "Valls, ciutat bressol dels castells" (Valls, the cradle of *castells*). There is a museum devoted to *castells* in the Plaça de Sant Roc.

THE MONASTERY OF SANTES CREUS

This monastery forms part of the "Cistercian Tour", along with those of Poblet and Vallbona de les Monges, in the neighbouring districts of Conca de Barberà and Urgell, respectively. It was founded in the 12th century, after the Christian Reconquest, when various nobles sponsored the creation of Cistercian monasteries to encourage resettlement of the area. Construction at Santes Creus began about 1150 under the patronage of the Montcada family, and with the protection of King Jaume I.

At present, the monastery of Santes Creus is the only one of the three that is not used for the purpose for which it was built. The last monks left in 1835 as a result of the laws depriving religious orders of their property. In 1921 it was declared to be part of the national historical heritage and afterwards restoration and preservation work began. Since 1975, concerts of classical and religious music have been held, as well as a course in Gregorian chant.

The gradual growth of the complex gave rise to buildings of various styles from the Romanesque to the Gothic. Overall, unlike the imposing grandeur of

Plaça Sant Bernat and the entrance to the church at the Santes Creus monastery.

Three views of the Santes Creus monastery: a view of the Gothic cloisters, the monastic lavatory in the pavilion at the centre of the cloisters and, below, the pointed arches in the back cloisters.

Poblet, this monastery is more artistically unified, with simpler and more severe forms.

In accordance with the rule of the order, there are three zones: the outer, where the labourers who cultivated the surrounding land lived, a second zone containing the abbot's palace and the hospital of the poor, while the third was devoted to monastic life proper. The second zone is entered through the gate of the Assumption, built in baroque style in the 18th century, which leads into the Plaça de Sant Bernat. The former hospice buildings are now private houses and the abbot's palace is the town hall of Aigamúrcia, the settlement established beside the monastery in the second half of the 19th century. In the centre of the square is a fountain with a monument to Sant Bernat Calbó, abbot of Santes Creus in the 13th century.

From this square the Royal Gate leads into the cloister of the monastery, from which the church can be entered. The church was the first building to be started, in 1168. It is characterised by its simple, austere lines. Inside there are the royal tombs of Pere II, Jaume II and the wife of the latter, Blanche of Anjou. From the church there is access to the former monks' dormitory.

Work on the cloister began in 1313, and was continued by the great mason Reinard des Fonoll, who gave it its characteristic ornamentation; the Flamboyant Gothic tracery of the windows and the capitals carved with a huge variety of motifs. In comparison, the second cloister is very austere and subdued. Also of great interest are the Royal Palace, built in the 13th century by Pere the Great, the sober, majestic chapter house, and the cellar, which still contains huge old wine barrels. The monastery's bibliographic archive is also very important.

General view of Vallbona de les Monges and a detail of the monastery cloisters.

THE MONASTERY OF VALLBONA DE LES MONGES

Although Vallbona is in fact in the province of Lleida, it is described here since it is not far from Poblet, and completes the Cistercian route. Of the three, it is the only one for nuns, although originally it housed a community of monks, who were not Cistercians. It seems this early community was not specifically linked to any order, but in 1175, with the arrival in Vallbona of a Cistercian abbess, it became a house of nuns and was attached to the Cistercian order.

The abbey of Vallbona de les Monges was built in marshy ground, where the difficulty of access favoured the distancing of the community of nuns from earthly matters. From the 16th century, the surrounding village began to be built, in accordance with the provisions of the Council of Trent, so as to protect the religious community from the attacks which it had suffered on a number of occasions.

Stylistically, the buildings at Vallbona are in general terms concordant with those of Santes Creus and Santa Maria de Poblet. The cloister is unusual in having an irregular, trapezoid shape, instead of being rectangular. It was built between the 12th and 14th centuries, and so contains both Romanesque and Gothic elements. Like the rest of the abbey, the chapter house perfectly reflects the order's austere spirit. It is presided by a 15th-century carving of the Virgin, which shows Renaissance influence.

The aisle-less, cruciform church was begun in the late 12th century. Its austerity, too, obeys Saint Bernard's dictates. It contains an image of the Virgin Mary, to whom it is dedicated, a beautiful Gothic carving by Guillem Seguer. Here too are the tombs of Violant d'Hungria, second wife of Jaume I, and of her daughter Sança d'Aragó. The penultimate bay of the nave is surmounted by an elegant octagonal lantern–bell tower.

The church, cloister and chapter-house are perfectly preserved. The abbey also contains excellent buildings from later periods, such as the present gate-house, parlour and guest-house, which date from the 18th century.

The square in front of the church at Santa Coloma de Queralt.

An attractive view of Carrer Piebania in Montblano.

MONTBLANC

The capital of the Conca de Barberà district stands on the river Francoli. It was a ducal city with a rich history, particularly in mediaeval times. It was declared a monument of historical and artistic interest in 1947. The town is surrounded by walls, built in the 14th century, of which some two thirds can still be seen, including 17 towers and two of the four original gateways, those of Sant Jordi and Bover. Amongst the notable buildings within the town are the majestic church of Santa Maria Major (14th to 16th centuries), with a facade remodelled in baroque style, in which an excellent 14th-century stone retable is preserved; the Gothic church of Sant Miquel, where the Corts Catalanes, the mediaeval Catalan parliament, met several times; the Royal Palace, a former residence of the monarchs of the Catalono-Aragonese dynasty; the church of Sant Marçal (14th century), which now contains the Frederic Marès museum of popular and liturgical art; the convent of La Sierra (14th century), the old hospital and the colonnaded Plaça Major, where the Desclergue palace stands.

SANTA COLOMA DE QUERALT

In this town so rich in ancient buildings, special mention should be made of the parish church (13th to 16th centuries) a beautiful example of Catalan Gothic which contains a valuable retable carved in stone by Jordi de Déu in 1380, and, on the outskirts, the sanctuary of Santa Maria de Bell-lloc, with its lovely 13th-century Romanesque doorway and the splendid tombs of the counts of Queralt, carved in alabaster in the 14th century. The quaint square known as Creu de les Canelles is also very interesting, with its 17th-century monumental fountain, beside which stands a beautiful Gothic cross, as are the remains of the old castle.

The church of Santa María de Poblet was built in the twelfth century, although the facade is seventeenth century.

THE MONASTERY OF SANTA MARIA DE POBLET

The monastery stands at the foot of the Prades hills, 3 km from l'Espluga del Francoli, a town of ancient origin, famous for the virtues of its ferrous waters which made it into an important spa.

Santa Maria de Poblet is the most monumental of the Catalan monasteries. It owes its origin to count Ramon Berenguer IV who, in 1151 after the reconquest of the area, donated some lands to the abbey of Montfreda for the building of a Cistercian monastery. In 1153 a community of monks settled there and work began. Most of the buildings were erected in the 12th and 13th centuries, and make up an extraordinarily beautiful architectural whole, gloriously set in the splendid countryside.

The monastery of Poblet, like that of Santes Creus, since they were both built by the Cistercian order, consists of three enclosures: the outer one, for the agricultural labourers, a second with a chapel, a hospital for the poor, a guest-house, the abbot's residence and store-rooms, and the third, walled, within which the monastic life proper is lived.

The second enclosure is entered by way of the 15th-century Porta Daurada. It contains the abbot's palace, the small Romanesque church of Santa Caterina and the Gothic chapel of Sant Jordi. On one side is the

A view of the Gothic palace of King Martí the Humane.

The Poblet monastery creates an architectural picture of outstanding beauty.

Porta Reial, built in the 14th century, which gives access to the monastic buildings, and the other is the doorway of the church, which is a large, austere 12th-century building with a 17th-century baroque facade, and includes side aisles, transepts and an apsidal east end. The alabaster Renaissance retable by Danià Forment is notable, as are the majestic tombs of the kings and queens of the Catalano-Aragonese dynasty in the crossing. Here lie Jaume I, the Conqueror, Pere IV the Ceremonious and his three wives, Alfons I, the Chaste Joan I and II with their wives Martí the Humane and Alfons the Magnanimous.

The cloister, erected in the 13th and 14th centuries, impregnated with beauty and serenity, is where the monastic atmosphere can perhaps be best appreciated. Also notable are the spacious refectory, from the 12th century, the monks' enormous dormitory, the 13th-century chapter house, with the graves of some of the abbots of Poblet, the 13th-century library, which contains important manuscripts and which, in the 14th century, was one of the most important in Europe, and the Gothic palace of King Martí the Humane.

The monastery of Poblet is not famous only for its great size or its legendary popular prestige, or indeed for its indisputable artistic and architectural worth, but also for its brilliant history as a community ruled by abbots of just renown.

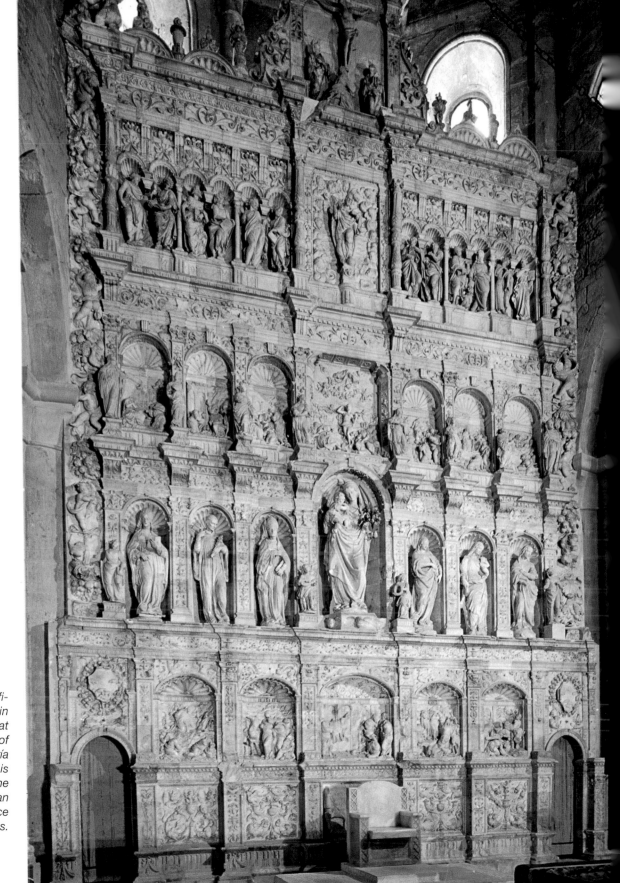

The magnificent main altarpiece at the church of Santa María de Poblet is one of the major Catalan Renaissance works.

Seen from the Romanesque church of Saint Mary in Siurana de Prada, there is a beautiful view of the mountains and plains of Siurana.

THE SERRA DE PRADES

The steep range of hills known as the Serra de Prades is rich in arboreal species, including holm oak, various other types of oak, pine and chestnuts. In the cultivated areas, mainly olives and hazel-nuts are grown. The fauna of Prades is typical of the coastal ranges, and includes large numbers of wild boar.

On a plateau in the centre of the range stands **Prades**. It is also known as "Villa Vermella" (the red town), because of the characteristic colour of its houses built from the reddish stone of the hills. Remains of the old town walls and the fortified gateway though which the town can be entered are testaments to its mediaeval

past. It was a very important place and the capital of a large county. Also interesting is the charming colonnaded square, which contains a spherical fountain in Renaissance style. The parish church of Santa Maria is an interesting building marking the transition from Romanesque to Gothic style.

Siurana de Prades is built on cliffs surrounded by precipices and appears to cling to an impressive escarpment. The surrounding area is singularly beautiful and the Siurana reservoir is nearby. The town was the last Moorish refuge in the province and was of great importance during the mediaeval period. Its splendid history stands in contrast to its decline at the begining of this century which culminated at one point

in its population being reduced to one sole inhabitant. It was at this point that restoration commenced on a large number of houses, thereby rescuing its particular charm from oblivion. In 1981 the town was declared part of the national historical and artistic patrimony. Amongst its buildings is a 12th century romanesque church.

The ruins of **Scala-Dei** are to be found in the neighbouring Serra de Montsant. Despite their ravaged appearance today, the few remains still standing are testimony to the solemnity of former times. It has its origins in the 12th century and its name, "ladder of God" would be the literal translation, refers to a shepherd who had a vision of a ladder leading to heaven. The best preserved structures are the main entrance and a small cloister. In 1980 it was declared part of the national historical and artistic patrimiony and restoration work comenced.

ESCORNALBOU

The Romans converted this 700 metre high pyramid-shaped mountain into a fortress to protect the mineral deposits in the area. In the 12th century the Augustinian canons built a fortified convent here, the castle of Sant Miquel d'Escornalbou. At the beginning of this century, due to its ruinous condition, restoration work commenced. Remains of the original building include the walls, with an ogival archway at the entrance, the 13th century church where Romanesque and Gothic styles converge and the Romanesque cloister. The most restored area is the convent which has beautiful rooms, especially the library which was founded by Eduard Toda who promoted the restoration work. The nearby Passeig dels Frares, or Friars' Way, which surrounds the monastery and the Santa Bárbara hermitage afford excellent vantage points from which to admire the castle and the mountains.

Nature and old centres of population give the landscape of the Serra de Prades a special attraction.

The castle of Sant Miquel d'Escornalbou.

CONTENTS

Collection ALL EUROPE

#	Title	Spanish	French	English	German	Italian	Catalan	Dutch	Swedish	Portuguese	Japanese	Finnish
1	ANDORRA	•	•	•	•	•	•				•	
2	LISBON	•	•	•	•	•				•		
3	LONDON	•	•	•	•	•					•	
4	BRUGES	•	•	•	•	•		•				
5	PARIS	•	•	•	•	•						
6	MONACO	•	•	•	•	•						
7	VIENNA	•	•	•	•	•						
11	VERDUN	•	•	•	•	•		•				
12	THE TOWER OF LONDON	•	•	•	•							
13	ANTWERP	•	•	•	•	•		•				
14	WESTMINSTER ABBEY	•	•	•	•	•						
15	THE SPANISH RIDING SCHOOL IN VIENNA	•	•	•	•	•				•		
16	FATIMA	•	•	•	•	•						
17	WINDSOR CASTLE	•	•	•	•	•					•	
19	COTE D'AZUR	•	•	•	•	•						
22	BRUSSELS	•	•	•	•	•		•				
23	SCHÖNBRUNN PALACE	•	•	•	•	•						
24	ROUTE OF PORT WINE	•	•	•	•	•				•		
26	HOFBURG PALACE	•	•	•	•	•						
27	ALSACE	•	•	•	•	•		•				
31	MALTA	•	•	•	•	•						
32	PERPIGNAN											
33	STRASBOURG	•	•	•	•	•						
34	MADEIRA + PORTO SANTO		•	•	•					•		
35	CERDAGNE - CAPCIR							•				
36	BERLIN	•	•	•	•	•						

Collection ART IN SPAIN

#	Title	Spanish	French	English	German	Italian	Catalan	Dutch	Swedish	Portuguese	Japanese	Finnish
1	PALAU DE LA MUSICA CATALANA	•					•					
2	GAUDI	•	•	•	•					•		
3	PRADO MUSEUM I (Spanish Painting)	•	•	•	•	•				•		
4	PRADO MUSEUM II (Foreign Painting)	•	•	•	•	•				•		
5	MONASTERY OF GUADALUPE	•	•	•	•							
6	THE CASTLE OF XAVIER	•	•	•	•							
7	THE FINE ARTS MUSEUM OF SEVILLE	•	•	•	•							
8	SPANISH CASTLES	•	•	•	•							
9	THE CATHEDRALS OF SPAIN	•	•	•	•							
10	THE CATHEDRAL OF GIRONA	•	•	•	•		•					
11	GRAN TEATRO DEL LICEO	•	•	•			•					
11	EL LICEO ARDE DE NUEVO	•	•	•			•					
12	THE CATHEDRAL OF CORDOBA	•	•	•	•	•						
13	THE CATHEDRAL OF SEVILLE	•	•	•	•							
14	PICASSO	•	•	•	•					•		
15	REALES ALCAZARES (ROYAL PALACE OF SEVILLE)	•	•	•	•							
16	MADRID'S ROYAL PALACE	•	•	•	•							
17	ROYAL MONASTERY OF EL ESCORIAL	•	•	•	•							
18	THE WINES OF CATALONIA	•										
19	THE ALHAMBRA AND THE GENERALIFE	•	•	•	•							
20	GRANADA AND THE ALHAMBRA	•	•	•	•							
21	ROYAL ESTATE OF ARANJUEZ	•	•	•	•							
22	ROYAL ESTATE OF EL PARDO	•	•	•	•							
23	ROYAL HOUSES	•	•	•	•							
24	ROYAL PALACE OF SAN ILDEFONSO	•	•	•	•							
25	HOLLY CROSS OF THE VALLE DE LOS CAIDOS	•	•	•	•							
26	OUR LADY OF THE PILLAR OF SARAGOSSA	•										
27	TEMPLE DE LA SAGRADA FAMILIA	•	•	•	•	•						
28	POBLET ABTEI	•	•	•	•		•					
29	MAJORCA CATHEDRAL	•	•	•	•	•	•					

Collection ALL SPAIN

#	Title	Spanish	French	English	German	Italian	Catalan	Dutch	Swedish	Portuguese	Japanese	Finnish
1	ALL MADRID	•	•	•	•	•					•	
2	ALL BARCELONA	•	•	•	•	•	•					
3	ALL SEVILLE	•	•	•	•	•						
4	ALL MAJORCA	•	•	•	•	•						
5	ALL THE COSTA BRAVA	•	•	•	•	•						
6	ALL MALAGA and the Costa del Sol	•	•	•	•	•						
7	ALL THE CANARY ISLANDS (Gran Canaria)	•	•	•	•	•		•	•			
8	ALL CORDOBA	•	•	•	•	•						
9	ALL GRANADA	•	•	•	•	•						
10	ALL VALENCIA	•	•	•	•	•						
11	ALL TOLEDO	•	•	•	•	•						
12	ALL SANTIAGO	•	•	•	•	•						
13	ALL IBIZA and Formentera	•	•	•	•	•						
14	ALL CADIZ and the Costa de la Luz	•	•	•	•	•						
15	ALL MONTSERRAT	•	•	•	•	•	•					
16	ALL SANTANDER and Cantabria	•	•	•	•	•						
17	ALL THE CANARY ISLANDS II (Tenerife)	•	•	•	•	•		•	•			•
20	ALL BURGOS	•	•	•	•	•			•			
21	ALL ALICANTE and the Costa Blanca	•	•	•	•	•						
22	ALL NAVARRA	•	•	•	•	•						
23	ALL LERIDA	•	•	•	•		•					
24	ALL SEGOVIA	•	•	•	•	•						
25	ALL SARAGOSSA	•	•	•	•	•						
26	ALL SALAMANCA	•	•	•	•	•			•			
27	ALL AVILA	•	•	•	•	•						
28	ALL MINORCA	•	•	•	•	•						
29	ALL SAN SEBASTIAN and Guipúzcoa	•										
30	ALL ASTURIAS	•	•	•								
31	ALL LA CORUNNA and the Rías Altas	•	•	•	•							
32	ALL TARRAGONA	•	•	•	•							
33	ALL MURCIA	•	•	•	•							
34	ALL VALLADOLID	•	•	•	•							
35	ALL GIRONA	•	•	•	•							
36	ALL HUESCA	•	•	•	•							
37	ALL JAEN	•	•	•	•							
40	ALL CUENCA	•	•	•	•							
41	ALL LEON	•	•	•	•							
42	ALL PONTEVEDRA, VIGO and the Rías Bajas	•	•	•	•	•						
43	ALL RONDA	•	•	•	•							
44	ALL SORIA	•	•									
46	ALL EXTREMADURA	•	•	•	•							
47	ALL ANDALUSIA	•	•	•	•							
52	ALL MORELLA	•	•	•	•							

Collection ALL AMERICA

#	Title	Spanish	French	English	German	Italian
1	PUERTO RICO	•		•		
2	SANTO DOMINGO	•		•		
3	QUEBEC			•	•	
4	COSTA RICA	•		•		
5	CARACAS	•		•		

Collection ALL AFRICA

#	Title	Spanish	French	English	German	Italian
1	MOROCCO	•	•	•	•	
2	THE SOUTH OF MOROCCO	•	•	•	•	
3	TUNISIA		•	•	•	
4	RWANDA		•			

SANTA COLOMA DE QUERALT

FORÉS

VENDRELL

MONTBLANC

SAN VICENTE
DE CALDERS

ESPLUGA DE FRANCOLÍ

MONASTERIO DE

SANTES

LA SELVA DE CAMP

CREUS

ALCOVER

VALLS

CUNIT

MONASTERIO DE POBLET

ALBINYANA

CALAFELL

PRADES

SEGUR DE CALA

SCALA DEI

SAN SALVADOR

COMARRUGA

REUS

TORREDEMBARR

FALSET

TARRAGONA

ALTAFULLA

ESCORNALBOU

SALOU

GANDESA

CAMBRILS

Río Ebro

PORT AVENTURA

L'AMETLLA DE MAR

TORTOSA

AMPOSTA

SAN CARLOS DE LA RÁPITA

ALCANAR

The printing of this book was completed
in the workshops of
FISA - ESCUDO DE ORO, S.A.
Palaudarias, 26 - Barcelona (Spain)